On My Way

written and illustrated by

Tomie dePaola

A 26 FAIRMOUNT AVENUE BOOK

PUFFIN BOOKS

PUFFIN BOOKS
Published by the Penguin Group
Penguin Putnam Books for Young Readers,
345 Hudson Street, New York, New York 10014, U.S.A.
Penguin Books Ltd, 80 Strand, London WC2R ORL, England
Penguin Books Australia Ltd, Ringwood, Victoria, Australia
Penguin Books Canada Ltd, 10 Alcorn Avenue, Toronto, Ontario, Canada M4V 3B2
Penguin Books (N.Z.) Ltd, 182-190 Wairau Road, Auckland 10, New Zealand

Penguin Books Ltd, Registered Offices: Harmondsworth, Middlesex, England

First published in the United States of America by G. P. Putnam's Sons,
a division of Penguin Putnam Books for Young Readers, 2001
Published by Puffin Books,
a division of Penguin Putnam Books for Young Readers, 2002

3 5 7 9 10 8 6 4 2

THE LIBRARY OF CONGRESS HAS CATALOGED THE G. P. PUTNAM'S SONS EDITION AS FOLLOWS:
DePaola, Tomie. On my way / written and illustrated by Tomie dePaola.
p. cm.—(A 26 Fairmount Avenue Book)
1. DePaola, Tomie—Childhood and youth—Juvenile literature.
2. DePaola, Tomie—Homes and haunts—Connecticut—Meriden—Juvenile literature.
3. Authors, American—20th century—Biography—Juvenile literature.
4. Meriden (Conn.)—Social life and customs—Juvenile literature.
5. Meriden (Conn.)—Biography—Juvenile literature.
[1. DePaola, Tomie—Childhood and youth.
2. Authors, American. 3. Illustrators.] I. Title. II. Series.
PS3554.E11474 Z477 2001 813'.54—dc21 [B] 00-038229
ISBN 0-399-23583-3

Puffin Books ISBN 0-698-11948-7

Printed in the United States of America

To Leah Grossman Caplan,
the best dancing teacher in the world,
and in loving memory of my mother, Flossie—
and, of course, to Mario,
who keeps me seeing so clearly.

Chapter One

Every spring my mom always said, "March comes in like a lion and goes out like a lamb." Well, this year March had come in like a lion all right—cold, wet, windy, and even snowy. But it certainly wasn't going out like a lamb.

Now it was almost the beginning of April and it was still cold, wet, and windy. Lots of kids were home with colds. Even some teachers were sick. Miss Luby, the school nurse, had a line waiting outside her office.

"Say *ahhhh!*" she'd say, sticking a small, smooth piece of wood called a tongue depressor in everyone's mouth (one at a time, of course).

Then she'd say, "You'd better go home until your throat gets better." Or, "Where's your handkerchief? Your nose is dripping." Or she would put the thermometer in your mouth, pull it out, and say, "My goodness, you have a temperature. Lie down on the cot until someone comes to get you."

I had the "sniffles," but nothing bad enough to keep me from going to school. Mom gave me a cup of hot Ovaltine every day when I got home. It was chocolaty-tasting and was supposed to be really good for "building you up." Little Orphan Annie drank it, too—on the radio.

I had to be careful not to get my feet wet so I wouldn't get a real cold. Buddy, my older brother, and I couldn't get close to our new baby sister, Maureen. After all, if we got colds, we didn't want to give them to the baby.

"I wish this weather would stop," Mom said. "All this damp and cold isn't good for the baby." The stove in our new house had a heater in it. So Mom closed the kitchen doors, turned the heater on, and kept Maureen in her carriage in the nice, warm kitchen. Mom would iron the clothes or cook the meals or sit at the kitchen table and read while rocking Maureen in her carriage.

But Maureen *did* catch a cold. She sneezed little baby sneezes. She coughed little baby coughs. Mom covered her in blankets and held her a lot, rocking her back and forth in her arms.

The doctor came and gave Mom some medicine for Maureen. Mom dipped a little cloth in the bottle and put it in Maureen's mouth to suck. She gave her vitamins and cod-liver oil with an eyedropper. But Maureen's cold didn't get any better!

When Dad came home from work, he would sit in the kitchen with Mom and my baby sister. I could tell they were worried. After all, Maureen was brand-new. She was only a couple of weeks old.

"Tomie, Buddy, wake up," Mom was calling. It was dark. I was a lighter sleeper than Buddy, so I woke up right away. I turned the light on next to my bed.

"Turn that light off," Buddy hollered from across the room.

"Mom's calling us," I said. "She wants us to get up." I was up and out the door to the hallway before Buddy had even gotten out of bed.

It was dark except for the little night-light in the bathroom. The long hallway to the stairs looked spooky.

I crept along, a little scared. The stairs went down into blackness. A tiny bit of light was coming from under the bottom of the kitchen door. I could hear Mom talking on the phone. She sounded upset. She was talking fast and a little loud. "What's going on?" Buddy asked, coming up behind me in the dark. I jumped.

"I don't know," I said. "Mom's really worried."

"Boys," she shouted, "come in the kitchen. Quick!" Mom was holding our baby sister, Maureen. She was all wrapped up in a baby blanket. Mom had her coat on. She was holding the car keys in her other hand. Maureen was breathing funny.

"Your father's at a meeting. Margaret Purcell is coming down to take care of you until your father gets home. As soon as Mrs. Purcell gets here, go back to bed." Mom rushed out the door. I ran to follow her, but Buddy stopped me.

I heard the car start, saw the headlights go on, and watched the car drive away. I called out, "Mom, what's happening?" But she was gone. I stood there looking after her.

In a little while, Mrs. Purcell came hurrying down the street and up the steps to the house.

"Okay, boys," she said, taking off her coat, "your mom wants you both to get back in bed."

5

She turned on the stair lights. Buddy pushed me up ahead of him into the bedroom. I waited until I heard him sleeping and crept out of bed, down the stairs.

"Tomie," Mrs. Purcell asked, "what are you doing up?"

"Where did Mom go with Maureen?" I asked.

"Come here, Tomie," Mrs. Purcell said. She held me and stroked my head. "Tomie, Maureen is very sick. Your mom had to take her to the hospital. Your dad's at a meeting, but he should be home soon. Do you want to sit with me until he gets here?"

"Yes," I said. Mrs. Purcell used to be a teacher. She and Mr. Purcell had a baby boy named Jimmy. He was a year older than Maureen, so she understood how scary it was that Maureen was sick.

"What book was your mom reading to you?" she asked.

"She was reading about Ali Baba and the Forty Thieves," I said, getting the book.

6

But I couldn't pay attention to the story. My mind kept wandering to the hospital.

The front door opened. It was Dad. "What's going on?" he asked when he saw Mrs. Purcell.

"Oh, Joe," she said, "Floss took Maureen to the hospital. She's awfully sick. She may have pneumonia. Jim said use our car. I can stay here with the boys."

"Daddy, can I come?" I cried.

"No, you have to stay here!" Dad answered. And off he went.

Mrs. Purcell got my pillow and a blanket from my bed. She let me curl up on the sofa.

"Mrs. Purcell, what's pneumonia?" I asked.

"It's like a really bad cold in your chest, Tomie. It makes it hard to breathe, especially for a little baby," she told me.

I was scared. Even more scared than I was of the dark.

Chapter Two

It was getting light out when Mom and Dad came home. They talked quietly with Mrs. Purcell.

"C'mon, Tomie," Dad said. "Go wash up and get ready for school. And wake up your brother, too."

When I came back down, Mom had some breakfast on the table. The empty carriage was still in the kitchen.

"Now, boys," Dad said when Buddy came in, "your baby sister is very, very ill. Mom and I will have to spend lots of time at the hospital. I'm going down to Wallingford this morning to get Aunt Nell to take care of you."

"I want you both to be good boys in school," Mom said, "and to mind Aunt Nell." Aunt Nell was my grandfather Tom's sister. Because all of her children were grown-ups, if there was ever a family crisis, Aunt Nell would show up to help in any way she could.

"I want to go with you to the hospital," I said.

Mom took me in her arms. She started to cry. "Oh, Tomie," she said, "just be a good boy and say lots of prayers for Maureen. I'll meet you in front of the hospital when school gets out"—the hospital was right across the street from the school— "and tell you how everything is. Okay?"

I had never seen Mom cry this hard before.

Miss Immick, the kindergarten teacher, was very nice to me. At Sunday school, Sister Mary Margaret asked the children to say a prayer for my baby sister.

Every night, Aunt Nell would help me say my prayers for Maureen. And when Mom and Dad got home from the hospital, Mom woke me up to tell me about Maureen.

My poor baby sister. She was so sick. She couldn't breathe by herself. Mom said she was being fed through a tube. It sounded awful.

But one good thing was, the doctors were using a new drug called sulfa. And that was supposed to help pneumonia.

More than a week went by. Mom and Dad looked tired. They spent as much time at the hospital as they could. Of course, Dad had to go to work, but Mom seemed to be there all day and night every day. She did see me every noontime and afternoon when school let out. She'd tell me the news.

It always seemed to be the same. "Maureen still needs help breathing. She's very weak, but they hope the sulfa drug is working. It's still too soon to tell."

A few nights later I heard a voice saying, "Tomie, Tomie." It was Mom gently shaking me. I looked up. Her face was covered with tears! *Oh NO!* I thought. *NO! NO!*

"Tomie, Maureen is going to be all right. She's out of danger. She can breathe by herself and she took her bottle, too! She's going to be all right!"

I held on to Mom and cried and cried. "Thank you, God," I whispered.

A few days later, Maureen came home from the hospital. She was in the same blanket that Mom had wrapped her up in to take her to the hospital. It became Maureen's "lucky blanket."

She looked very small, but the doctor had said that she was a strong baby to have gotten over pneumonia. She was only a month and a few days old.

Everybody in the family was so happy. Especially me!

Chapter Three

Well, I guess good news changes every-thing, even the weather. The sun came out, flowers started to poke up through the ground, birds were singing. I pretended the whole world was happy that my  baby sister was better and back home. And it was al-most time for our summer vacation. School would be over soon. I couldn't wait to get out of kindergarten and into first grade.

One Saturday morning, Mom was reading the newspaper while we were eating break-fast. "Oh my," she said, "the World's Fair might not reopen in September. I'm glad we went to see it last fall. I hope you remember it all, Tomie. It's a part of history. When you grow up, you'll find out that to remember things that you've done as a little boy is part of your history."

The thing was, I remembered *everything*, especially our trip to the World's Fair.

It all began one day last fall when my mom met me after school. I had just started kindergarten.

"We're going shopping for a new outfit," she told me.

We walked to Perlin's, the children's clothing store. I had already started school and I had a new outfit. I knew it wasn't Easter. I always got a new outfit then, too. This was obviously some other special occasion.

I tried on lots of clothes. The saleslady, whose name was Goldie, kept bringing stuff out. "I know," she said, "I have just the thing." She went to the back of the store and came out with a dark green outfit. It had a pair of overalls, a short jacket, and a cap with a brim.

13

"It's gabardine—and it's water-repellent,"
Goldie told my mom. "Put a cute striped jer-
sey under it and he'll be the best-dressed boy
at the World's Fair."

The World's Fair—were we going? No one
had said anything about it. I couldn't
believe it.

"Are we really going?" I asked Mom on the
way home.

"Yes, I was trying to keep it a secret, but
Goldie's got a big mouth! Never mind, we
are going!"

The 1939 New York World's Fair had
opened last summer. It was supposed to be

the most exciting event in years. They even built a new highway from New Haven, Connecticut, to New York just so people could get there quickly.

I never thought we'd really go to it. I had a pretty good idea of what the World's Fair looked like. I had seen it in newsreels at the movies and pictures of it in magazines. Two buildings were the "symbol" for the fair. The Perisphere was in the shape of a big ball. The Trylon looked like a tall pointed thing. But what I really wanted to see was Futurama, the World of Tomorrow, in the General Motors Pavilion.

Mom also took Buddy to Besse-Boynton's, which sold men's and older boys' clothes, to get a new outfit.

He ended up with some woolen knickers (pants that came to your knees) and knee socks with diamond patterns on them. He had a new woolen sports jacket and a hat. He looked pretty grown-up.

We were going to go in two cars—ours and Uncle Charles's. There would be Mom, Dad, Buddy, Uncle Charles, his girlfriend, Viva, their friend Mickey Lynch, Tom, my grandfather, and me. We were going on a Sunday. We were to meet at Holy Trinity Church in Wallingford to go to the first mass at 5:30 A.M. Then we'd leave right away. It would take about three hours.

On Saturday night, Mom went to Alexander's, the candy store, and bought a huge bag of popcorn for me. I got carsick all the time and the doctor said that eating popcorn would help. And it did. It was just plain—no butter, no salt. Buddy was jealous. It was all *mine*!

After church the grown-ups decided that Buddy would ride with Uncle Charles, his girlfriend, Viva, and Mickey Lynch. I would ride with Mom, Dad, and Tom.

Away we went, happy as could be. We didn't even mind the cloudy sky.

But then on the way it started to sprinkle. Mom said what Nana Upstairs always said,

"Rain before seven, clear before eleven." It was before seven, so that was great.

We stopped on the Merritt Parkway to get gas, and Buddy and I changed places. I took my popcorn. I was eating it *very* slowly so it would last. It was still raining. And it was still raining when we pulled into the big parking lot in Flushing Meadows.

"We're here!" Mom said. We were really at the World's Fair. "It's too bad it's raining so hard. We won't see Cousin Morton."

Our cousin Morton was Morton Downey, the famous Irish tenor. At the fair, he sang at Billy Rose's Aquacade, a big water show with swimmers. But the theater was outside. All the seats were wet. There wasn't going to be a show that day.

With such bad weather, everyone was getting wet, but I was *water-repellent*. The grown-ups bought umbrellas, which helped a little. But there was a plus! The lines for all the attractions weren't long, so we went into lots of exhibits.

We went to Ripley's Believe It or Not and saw a two-headed cow. We saw Elsie the Cow in the Borden's Pavilion. She was very pretty—for a cow.

We visited Singer's Midget Village. Lots of these little people had been Munchkins in the movie *The Wizard of Oz.*

We went into their little houses. All the grown-ups had to scoot down low. Uncle Charles and his girlfriend, Viva, were too tall, so they didn't go into any of the little houses. They were just the right size for me. I saw a little lady ironing and a little man in a little armchair

reading a little newspaper. But they weren't dressed in their Munchkin costumes.

Soon it was time for lunch. The grown-ups had decided to go to a fancy French restaurant. It was all pink mirrors and lots of waiters in tuxedos like Dad wore when he and Mom went out to the Elks Club on New Year's Eve.

Uncle Charles said, "Okay, boys, you can have *anything* you want."

I couldn't read yet, but I looked at the big menu anyway.

"Where does it say 'pancakes and sausages'?" I asked. That was my favorite food at the time.

"I don't see hamburgers," Buddy said.

The waiter was nice, but he said that wasn't the kind of food they served. He told us about a children's restaurant that wasn't too far away. They had food we kids liked, and famous characters who cooked and served it.

"I'll take them," Mom said. "You all stay here and enjoy yourselves."

"No, you'll get lost, Floss. I'll come with you," Uncle Charles said.

"Well, I'm not staying here," Viva said. "I'll come, too!"

"Me, too," Dad said.

"Count me in," Mickey Lynch said.

"Well, they don't have corned beef and cabbage, either," Tom said.

So out we all went back into the rain, and trooped down to the children's restaurant.

The Lone Ranger was making sandwiches with Wonder Bread. (They sponsored his radio show. That meant they paid for it.) Aunt Jemima was making my pancakes and Wimpy (from Popeye) made my brother's hamburger. Little Orphan Annie was serving

Ovaltine. It was so much fun and we had a great time.

"Well," Dad said, "it's time to go."

Everyone stood up and put on their jackets and hats.

"Someone stole my hat!" Buddy said. The hat he put on his head was too small!

"Oh dear," Viva said. Her skirt was a little above her knees. So was Mom's. All the sleeves on their jackets were too short. Everyone's woolen clothes had shrunk from all the rain—except mine! My water-repellent outfit did just fine.

What a funny-looking group we were when we went to see the Westinghouse Robot. It was very tall and made out of shiny metal.

A man would ask the robot questions and it would answer!

"All of us should be dressed like him," Tom said. "Then we wouldn't have shrunk."

Next we went to see Dunninger on stage. He could read minds. He was blindfolded when they brought him out on the stage. He stood with his back to the audience and started answering questions before anyone even asked them.

Then Dunninger told the audience to concentrate on something. It got very quiet. I thought about learning to read. Then Dunninger spoke. "There is a lady in  the front row wearing a very unusual necklace. It is made out of painted pinecones."

"That's me!" Mom shouted out.

"We just have time to see Futurama before the fireworks start," Dad said when we got outside.

We stood in line until it was our turn. We went inside and there was the world and the cities the way they might be in the

22

future, with automatic highways and big, tall buildings with places on top for helicopters to land. I loved it.

We went outside and Tom lifted me onto his shoulders. The rain had stopped. Then the fireworks started.

One after the other, bursting in the air, it was the best and longest fireworks show I had ever seen.

I don't remember driving home. I must have fallen fast asleep. But you can be sure I dreamt all about the 1939 New York World's Fair. I was hoping we'd go back on a day when the sun was out.

But we never did.

Chapter Four

I had started going to Miss Leah's Dancing School last September. I was taking Beginning Tap. First we had learned all kinds of steps and then a tap number (that's a dance putting all the steps together). Miss Leah called it a military tap. We would do it in the recital at the end of May in the auditorium of the Meriden City Hall with the whole city watching.

There were ten girls in the class and two boys—me and a boy named Joey. In the recital we would all dress as wooden toy soldiers.

Joey and I were going to wear white satin pants with a gold stripe down each leg; red satin jackets with gold buttons, gold braid, and little "brushes" on the 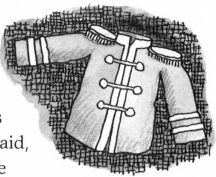 shoulders called epaulets; and tall hats with little visors and feathered things on the front. Our tap shoes would be painted white.

Mom was good at sewing, but for such an important occasion a seamstress lady was going to make *all* the costumes so they would *all* look alike.

I was also going to do a special number with Joan Ciotti, Miss Leah's star pupil. (She was a year older than I was.) We would dance together as the Farmer in the Dell and his wife in the part of the recital called "Nursery Rhyme Time." Our music was the song "Reuben, Reuben, I've been thinking . . ."

I had to practice singing, too. Miss Leah had written new words to "The Farmer in the Dell." She wanted me to sing them to introduce our dance number.

One day after practice, Miss Leah said to me and Joan, "Here is a picture of what you will wear for the recital. It's called a costume sketch."

Then she explained that the picture had been painted just for us by a store in New York City. They sold fabric and stuff used in famous musicals on Broadway—and for Miss Leah's recitals, of course!

"The costumes are beautiful," my mom told Miss Leah.

Joan would wear a short blue satin skirt with lots of petticoats, a green-and-white striped blouse and kerchief, and a white ruffled apron with orange trim.

My costume was a blue satin short-sleeved shirt, green-and-white striped overalls with big orange buttons, and an orange handkerchief in the back pocket. I would have on a straw hat with a blue band around it.

"How are you going to make my beard?" I asked.

"Your beard?" Mom and Miss Leah asked.

"Yes," I said. "The Farmer in the Dell in my nursery rhyme book has a little beard on his chin."

Mom and Miss Leah had a "conference."

"All right," Miss Leah said to my mom, "if you can figure out how to do it." And Mom did!

The recital was going to be on Saturday night. On Wednesday after school, our tap class went to City Hall for our first practice. Miss Leah called it a rehearsal. That made it sound like the real thing! Miss Leah showed us the stage and explained about the lights and the curtains. Then we rehearsed. It was so exciting.

But Saturday morning would be even more exciting. We had to be there for a real dress rehearsal. That's when we would do the whole recital in our costumes for the first time. All the other dancers from Miss Leah's Dancing School would be there.

Friday afternoon, disaster struck. Mom got a phone call from the seamstress lady's sister.

27

It seemed that the seamstress lady had had a "shock." I had no idea what that was, only that she was sick. She had all the costumes done—except for my military costume!

Mom said she would finish it. It was a good thing that Mom knew how to sew. There were buttons and braid and the feather on the hat to sew on. It would take time.

"Okay, Tomie," Mom said, "you won't have your military costume at the dress rehearsal because it won't be finished. But don't worry, I will have it ready for the performance."

So, at the dress rehearsal I was the only soldier in my practice shorts and shirt. The kids were afraid to ask where my costume was. I decided I would tell them a "fib."

"We're too poor," I said. I saw Mom listening. "I'm only kidding," I said quickly. "It won't be ready until tonight."

Of course, my farmer costume was ready—just waiting for me to hop into it. Mom took some cotton batting from a box. She cut out a little white beard shape and put some white adhesive tape at the top of it so it wouldn't come apart at the edges. "Chew," she said as she stuck some chewing gum in my mouth. When the chewing gum was ready, she stuck some on my chin and stuck the beard to it. "Move your face and mouth," she said. I did. The beard stayed right in place.

One of the little girls from the baby class came by and stopped and looked. *"Oooo,"* she said, "has you got a *boo-boo?"*

The dress rehearsal was so exciting, with all the dance numbers, the music, the lights, the scenery, the costumes. Everything we had been doing in Miss Leah's dance studio suddenly made real sense on the stage.

When we weren't performing, we sat in the audience and watched all the other numbers. Toe dancing, acrobatics, tap, and toe-tap.

A girl tapped while she was on her toes—WOW! Another girl bent over backward and

picked up a flower in her teeth. An older boy—just a year older than me—danced with a girl, just the two of them. Their dance was more like

Mr. Fred Astaire and Miss Ginger Rogers twirling around the stage, just like in the movies.

That afternoon Mom made me take a nap while she sewed my military costume.

But I was too excited to sleep. I just lay there, waiting for the big night.

Mom sewed on the last gold button. It was time to go.

When we got to the auditorium, we went backstage. All the mothers were putting lipstick and rouge on the kids' faces.

Mom started on mine. *"Blot,"* Mom said, holding a piece of tissue between my lips.

"Good," she said, "not too bright."

"Military tap next," Miss Leah's cousin Rhoda called out. We all lined up. I was the first one out on the stage. The lights hit me! I was in heaven. I did everything just right. One funny thing, though. Joey kept on trying to see who the kid in the costume at the other end of the line was. He thought I'd be wearing my practice clothes. So he thought I was someone else.

There was time between the military tap and the nursery rhyme scene. Mom changed my costume. I chewed the gum. The beard went on.

Joan Ciotti and I stood, waiting to go on. Mrs. Anderson began playing our music on the piano. Joan and I stepped into the big spotlight and danced over to the center of the stage. The audience began to laugh and to clap before we had done anything.

I stepped forward and sang my song. The audience clapped again—even louder this time.

Joan and I danced, smiling at the audience and at each other. We didn't make one mistake! We loved every minute of it.

We finished and took our bows. I heard clapping and whistling. Joan and I left the stage. Miss Leah was standing there. "You were wonderful!" she said. "Go out and take another bow." We did. In fact, we ended up taking *three* more bows.

I was bitten by the show-business bug! Maybe I'd go to Hollywood and dance and sing with Shirley Temple, my favorite movie star!

Chapter Five

It was the very last week of school. Kindergarten would soon be over and *real school* would begin in September. Like everyone else in the class, I wanted to know which first grade teacher I would get, Miss Delaney or Miss Kiniry.

I wanted Miss Kiniry. She was pretty and she'd smile and say hello to me on Sundays at church. She went to St. Joseph's, too. So, every day I waited for Miss Immick to tell us whose first grade we'd be in.

That last week was very busy! We had a big assembly in the schoolyard. Miss Fesiden, the lady who came and taught Folk Dancing, had each class perform a different

dance—a minuet, a square dance, the Virginia reel. We kindergartners had to do "London Bridge Is Falling Down." How dumb! (What would Miss Leah think if she saw me?) Oh well, only a few more days!

Finally it was the last day of school. We would only be there in the morning. We went into our own rooms and sat on our chairs. Miss Immick stood in front of us. She read off the names of everyone who was going on to first grade. Everyone "passed." No one was left out. *That's good*, I thought. *I guess everyone has learned how to PLAY. Great! We can get to reading at last.*

"Now," she said, "when school begins in September, come back to this room. Then we will find out which first grade class you'll be in. It will be a big surprise! I hope you all have a wonderful summer!"

The bell rang and school was over.

Jeannie Houdlette, my best friend, came over with Carol Crane from Columbus Avenue, where we used to live. We always walked home together.

"Wait a minute," I said. "I have to ask Miss Immick something."

"Yes, Tommy," Miss Immick said. (All the teachers in the school made me spell my name T-O-M-M-Y instead of T-O-M-I-E.)

"Do you know who I'm going to have for first grade? I won't tell that you told me," I pleaded.

"Oh, Tommy," she said, smiling. "It's not decided yet. We will have a meeting later on to make up the list. Now, run along. And don't forget, have a wonderful summer!"

"It's not fair," I said to Jeannie and Carol. "We have to wait *all summer*. It's not fair."

Jeannie just looked at me. I guess she didn't care which teacher she got. But I sure did. September was a long way off.

Chapter Six

When Jeannie and I got home from school, Mr. Johnny Papallo and some of his friends were standing outside our house with my dad. "They must be here to help with the wall and Mom's steps!" I said.

Ever since we had moved to the new house, Dad had been talking about a wall and Mom had been talking about steps.

"We need a wall to hold the front yard in place," Dad said.

"I just want real steps and not those wooden ones up to the front door," Mom said.

We had moved to 26 Fairmount Avenue in the middle of winter when the ground was too frozen for anyone to work. We had been walking from the street up to the house on wooden planks.

That weekend the men mixed cement to make concrete for the walk and the steps. I watched them pour the cement for the walk. Mr. Papallo came over. "Would you like to put your initials in the corner of the walk, Tomie?"

I would!

"Now your name will be there as long as the walk is there," Mr. Papallo told me.

That night Uncle Charles and his girl-friend, Viva, came over for dinner. I told him about my initials in the walk.

"You're just like a movie star," Uncle Charles said. He told me that there was a famous movie theater in Hollywood. Movie stars put their handprints, their footprints, and their names in the cement in front of the theater— just like this.

The next morning, when no one was looking, I went outside and pushed my hands into the cement. I was too late. It was already hard. But I still felt a little like a movie star.

"More good news!" Dad said, coming out of the house. "We're going to start the wall today."

A truck arrived and dumped a huge pile of rocks in front of the yard. Dad's friends came and set up wooden stakes with string stretched along where the wall would go. This would keep the wall even as they built it. They used a small cement mixer to mix the cement, and the wall was begun. Rock after rock it went up.

"It's going to be beautiful," Mom said.

Every day the neighbors stood around and watched. Sometimes one of them would say, "No, no, not that rock next. This one."

Dad's friends who were building the wall ignored them. "Sidewalk superintendents," they would say quietly under their breaths.

When they finished the wall, the men made a real sidewalk between the wall and the street.

Great, I thought. *When I learn to roller-skate, I'll have a place to practice.* (The only trouble was that for a very long time ours was the only piece of sidewalk on Fairmount Avenue!)

Now that we had the wall, the steps, and the sidewalk, the driveway was next. The hill up to the garage was very steep. A big truck came and poured tar and stones on it.

The tar and stones had to be packed down. Dad could pay a man with a steamroller to come. But he decided to do it himself with a hand roller to save money. (Mom was not so sure this was a good idea.)

But when Dad started rolling, it was not easy. (Every once in a while my dad used some bad words. That day he used more than ever!)

He tried pushing the roller up. He tried pulling the roller up. He huffed and he puffed. But every time the roller rolled back down before he could get it all the way up the hill.

All of a sudden I had an idea.

"Hey, Daddy, why don't you tie some rope to the handle of the roller? You could pull it up and then let it down."

Dad stopped and looked at me. "Hey, Tomie, you sure learned a lot in school this year!" He called my mom. "Floss, can you come out and help me?"

When they had
the roller ready
to go, Dad and
Mom grabbed
the rope. Dad
yelled, "Heave!"
and they pulled.
"Heave!" and
they pulled.

It worked.
I was so proud!

Our new tar-and-
stone driveway was

called "blacktop." It only had one problem.
Dad had made it so smooth by rolling it that
it was really slippery. If you had leather soles
on your shoes, you could stand at the top and
slide all the way down. I didn't, but Buddy
did. And so did some of the grown-ups.

Sometimes the car wouldn't make it all
the way up. The tires would spin and the car
would slip backward. Mom and Dad had to
get a running start from across the street to
make it to the top.

But Buddy and I loved the driveway. He'd sail down on his shoes and I'd race down in my red wagon or fly down so fast in my metal airplane that I thought I was really flying. Sometimes I tipped over at the bottom and skinned my knees in the gravel on the street. (It's a good thing there weren't many cars on our street, because we couldn't stop without going into the street.) Finally, Mom couldn't stand it any longer.

"Joe, you have to get that driveway fixed. Someone is going to get hurt."

Dad made a phone call, and a man arrived in a truck. He took one look and said, "Ya rolled it too much. Ya made it smooth as glass. I can fix it, but it'll cost ya!"

I put my fingers in my ears. I thought Dad might just explode. But he didn't. He and the man talked. They were both *Paisanos*—both Italians—so they made a deal.

The next day the truck came back with more tar and stones and with a small steamroller. In no time, the driveway was fixed.

No more slipping and sliding. No more racing and flying.

Chapter Seven

That first summer on Fairmount Avenue I really wanted to go exploring the neighborhood like Buddy did on his bike. But I was only five, going on six, so I wasn't allowed to go very far. Mom did let me cross the street, though, and go through two backyards to Jeannie's house.

Mr. and Mrs. Conroy lived next door to the Houdlettes. The Nadiles lived next door to the Conroys. Mr. Conroy and Mr. Nadile were teachers like Mr. Houdlette, Jeannie's father. The Nadiles had two daughters, Paulette and Sheila. Paulette was older than Buddy, and Sheila was younger than I was.

Lots of kids lived in the neighborhood.

Early one evening after supper, Mom invited a whole bunch of them to our house to play.

"How would everyone like to play a great game?" Mom asked the crowd of kids. They were all different ages.

"Yes, yes," they answered.

"All right," Mom said, "everyone go and find a special thing like a white rock, or a flower, or a leaf. Whatever you want. It's going to be your own forfeit."

"What's a forfeit?" I asked.

"It is the thing you give me to get something else," Mom told me. "Just go and find something. You'll see how it works."

Everyone rushed around and got what they wanted for their forfeit. No two forfeits could be the same.

When we were all back with our forfeits, Mom said, "Stand in a circle." She stood in the middle, closed her eyes, and turned around and around. She stopped and pointed at someone. It was Paulette Nadile.

"Okay, I'm IT," Mom said. "Paulette, you are the forfeit holder. I'm going to sit here on the back steps. You stand behind me with all the forfeits so I can't see them. Hold them over my head, one at a time, and say, 'Forfeit, forfeit. What should this forfeit do?'"

Paulette picked up a red flower and held it over Mom's head. It was Jeannie's. "Sweep the front steps," Mom told her. Jeannie groaned.

"Do a funny dance." "Pick up the clothespins." "Put the rake in the garage," Mom said as Paulette held the forfeits over her head.

The kids weren't sure if this was a fun game or not. Then Mom said, "Go into the kitchen and get a piece of cake." And, "Go to the refrigerator and get a Kool-Aid popsicle."

Everyone had a great time. Even though you might have to sweep the stairs, you might also get a piece of cake.

Some of the other games Mom showed us how to play were "Drop the clothespins into the milk bottle" and "Roll down the hill in the backyard." Mom knew so many games. All the kids loved to come to our house.

Once I heard Mrs. Conroy say to Mom, "Floss, I don't know how you do it—so many kids."

"Well," Mom said, "at least I know where my kids are!"

I got beginner roller skates that summer. They tied on and I didn't need a skate key the way "real," ball-bearing roller skates did. The wheels didn't turn that fast, but it was a way to get used to roller-skating.

Dad said, "You know, I wouldn't be surprised if you got a pair of ball-bearing roller skates for your birthday." (My birthday was September 15.)

It was almost the Fourth of July when Dad said, "Okay, boys, hop in the car. We're going down to Tracy to get some fireworks."

Tracy was a little town between Meriden and Wallingford. The people in Tracy were allowed to sell fireworks once a year for the Fourth.

Lots of booths were set up in front of the houses, filled with all kinds of fireworks to buy. Chinese firecrackers in beautiful little packages of colored tissue with strange designs on them, skyrockets, pinwheels, Roman candles.

"Hey, Dad," Buddy yelled. "This is the cap pistol I want." Dad bought it for him. I was "too young" to have one.

But Dad said, "C'mon, Tomie, help me pick out some pinwheels and fountains."

We went from booth to booth, filling up bags. "Daddy, will you buy me some Black Snakes?" They were my favorites. Black Snakes were little black "pills."

When a grown-up lit them with a match, they would grow into these long, black snaky things with lots of smoke around them.

We had a Fourth of July picnic. Carol Crane and her parents came up from Columbus Avenue, and other friends from the new neighborhood were there, too. We ate hot dogs and hamburgers.

"Floss, you make the best clam chowder in the world," Carol Crane's father said.

Soon it began to get dark. Dad passed out sparklers, and they lit up the lawn like birthday candles.

Then our dads shot off skyrockets from empty milk bottles, pinwheels, fountains, and all kinds of fireworks.

"Keep moving that Roman candle in circles," Mr. Houdlette said to Mr. Conroy.

"Are there any more pinwheels?" Mr. Nadile asked.

"Stay back, kids," my dad called out to Jeannie and me.

Then the city fireworks began. Even though they were shot off in the park on Lewis Avenue, we could see them really well because our house was on a hill.

I liked the finale best of all—lots of rockets and lots of big bangs. The sound echoed all around the hills surrounding Meriden.

Chapter Eight

For as long as I could remember, we drove down to the beach at Hammonasset in the summer. It was on Long Island Sound, the Connecticut side. And it was salt water.

A few days after the Fourth, Mom said, "Tomie and Buddy, we're going to the beach tomorrow. Be sure and get everything ready before you go to bed."

"Okay, Mom," I said. I raced upstairs and got my bathing suit, towel, pail, and shovel for playing in the sand.

The next morning, we packed the car with all our stuff, the beach umbrella, and the food. On the way out of Meriden we stopped at the icehouse to buy a block of ice to keep the food and drinks cold.

Then we were on our way!

Mom and Dad liked to get there early so we'd have a good parking place at Meig's Point. It was at the far end of the park. Dad always tried to park in front of a bathhouse. This was a little building where you could change into or out of your bathing suit.

As soon as we got there, Buddy and I jumped out of the car and ran into the bathhouse to change. Then we ran right down to the water and waited for Mom and Dad.

"Hold my hands," Mom said when we got into the water. She swished me around and around, making waves.

Then I made castles in the sand with my beach bucket until it was time to eat.

"Lunchtime!" Mom yelled. We got under the beach umbrella and ate our sandwiches and drank Kool-Aid.

"Let's walk down the beach to the boardwalk," Dad said.

"Hurray!" I said. I knew this meant we would get ice cream.

The only trouble was that on the way back Mom always said, "You have to wait *one* hour before you can go swimming again. If you don't, you'll get a cramp."

We stayed until the sun got lower in the sky. Then we packed up, changed out of our bathing suits, and headed home.

On the way, we stopped at Madison Pines, a little park, to finish up the rest of the food.

I fell asleep on the way home just like I always did. I would have liked to go to Hammonasset every day, but it was too far away.

Hammonasset wasn't the only beach we went to. Our uncle Frank had a cottage in Tiverton, Rhode Island. It was right on the water at a place we called "The Hummocks."

Every summer when Dad had his vacation from the barbershop, we went there for a week. The cottage was right on the beach. Uncle Frank had a rowboat, and Dad would take Buddy and me out rowing. I learned to dive—well, actually to jump off the boat into the water where Dad would catch me.

Uncle Frank lived in Fall River, Massachusetts, with Aunt Susie and my cousins Frances and Connie. My aunt Clorinda (my dad's sister) and my Italian grandmother, Nana Fall-River, lived there, too. (That's why we called her Nana Fall-River.)

Every afternoon Uncle Frank and Aunt Susie brought Nana Fall-River down in the car. Nana Fall-River loved to swim. The first thing she did was to get into her bathing suit. It looked like a big black dress.

She would go right down to the water, bless herself, splash water on her face and arms, and plunge in. She'd float on her back, her big black dress billowing up around her. She would float and float and float for what seemed like hours.

I thought it was great to have a grandmother who went swimming. Nana Downstairs, my Irish grandmother, didn't even go to the beach. Once I asked Jeannie if either of her grandmothers went swimming. She said they didn't. I thought that I was lucky.

One summer when I was younger, Aunt Clotilda and her son, Frankie, came to Uncle Frank's cottage with us. As soon as we got out of the car, Frankie and I ran down to the beach and ran back yelling, "The beach is full of rocks! Our feet hurt."

"I know," my cousin Frances said. "I bought you boys these rubber bathing shoes to wear. You can walk right into the water in them."

Frances and Connie had come down with Nana Fall-River for the day. They wore bathing caps to keep their hair from getting wet. They didn't want to spoil their hairdos when they went swimming. "Frankie and I want bathing caps, too," I told my mother.

Sure enough, Frances had bought caps for Frankie and me. They didn't fit too well, but we didn't care. We wore them anyway.

Frankie and I had a great time together. Dad taught us to "swim" between his legs. We didn't really swim. We'd pull ourselves along through the water by reaching down to the bottom and using our hands.

We loved Uncle Frank's cottage—except for one thing. It didn't have a bathroom with a shower and a toilet in it. We had to shower outside and the water was always cold. And if we had to go, we had to use the outhouse. This was a little hut. Inside was a wooden bench with a hole in the middle. You didn't flush. You just went. It was always stinky. I held my nose the whole time I was in there. So did Frankie.

"*Ahhh*," Buddy said. "Just get a clothespin for your noses, you babies!"

Chapter Nine

Summer was almost over. In a few days it would be Buddy's birthday party. On August 31 he'd be ten years old. (I was going to be six, two weeks later.)

This year, not only were his old friends from Columbus Avenue coming, but his friends in the new neighborhood.

"I'm too old to have one of those dress-up parties," Buddy said. Our birthday parties were always dress-up parties. Mom called them "masquerade parties."

"Okay," Mom said. "You don't have to if you don't want to." I was disappointed.

That night after supper, I asked Dad, "Can we watch the movies of our birthdays?" Dad had a movie camera, and he or Mom always took movies of our birthdays and anything else that was going on in our lives!

"Sure, Tomie. That would be fun," Dad said.

We started looking at a movie of Buddy's birthday party. There I was at three, all dressed up as Shirley Temple. Carol Crane was a clown. Bobby Brooks was a skeleton. The Fournier brothers were dressed up like ladies. Buddy was Joe Palooka, the comic book prizefighter, complete with a black eye. We were all eating ice cream and cake and waving at the camera. Buddy was biting into the biggest piece of watermelon you ever saw!

I remember everything about that day, especially "The Wedding."

Our mothers had wanted do a "Tiny Tot Wedding." They got the idea from a Little Rascals movie. Buddy's birthday was the perfect time to do it. The house and yard were all decorated with crepe paper and balloons. The wedding could be the entertainment. Everyone at the birthday party would be the wedding guests. They even invited a reporter from the newspaper, and she was coming.

Carol Crane was going to be the bride because she was the tallest girl. Mom thought that Buddy would be the groom.

"I'm not going to be in a stupid make-believe wedding," Buddy said. "It's my birthday, so I don't have to do it."

"All right," Mom said. They would just ask someone else. But the mothers didn't know that Buddy got all the other boys to say no, too!

"Maybe Tomie can be the groom," Mrs. Crane said. "We have to find someone quickly. The newspaper's coming."

"I'm too short to be a groom," I said. That was true, since I was only three.

After a lot of talking and rushing around, one of the mothers got an idea. Everyone in the Tiny Tot Wedding rushed up to the Adams house to get ready.

Neighbors lined the sidewalk. The lady reporter was there. The "Tiny Tot Bridal Party" would walk from the Adams house down the sidewalk to our house. The wedding ceremony would be performed in the garage. It was decorated with flowers, colored ribbons, and candles.

Everett Adams pulled his wagon with the wind-up record player playing "Here Comes the Bride." A little flower girl led the way.

Next came the bridesmaids in long dresses and carrying flowers. The bride, wearing a lace curtain for a veil, came last.

They marched down to our house. The groom was waiting. Wow! Carol Crane made a really great groom. All her red curls were hidden underneath one of her dad's hats. She wore pants and a jacket with a flower in the buttonhole.

After the ceremony in the garage, the wedding party came outside to have their pictures taken. Mom had the home movie camera going all the time.

Buddy was just standing there watching

with a glum look on his face. He wasn't happy that his birthday was ending with a Tiny Tot Wedding.

"Oh," the lady reporter said, looking at the bride. "How cute. Who is that pretty little bride?" she asked Buddy.

"That bride is my brother!"

Chapter Ten

The first day of school arrived! I was excited and nervous all at once.

We got to school and the bell rang. We all lined up by class. Last year's sixth-graders were not there. They had gone to Lincoln Junior High School.

We filed into Miss Immick's room.

"Well, hello, boys and girls," she said. "I hope we all had a wonderful summer vacation."

Another bell rang. We stood at attention and recited the Pledge of Allegiance to the flag. Then Miss Immick had us all sit down on the floor. It had been polished until it shone like a mirror.

On the first day of school everything was clean and shiny and smelled of floor wax and lemon oil polish. The blackboards were the cleanest they'd be all year. The waxed wooden floors in the hallways squeaked when you walked on them.

The first day of school was always special to me. I wondered when we would find out which first grade we were in. But I didn't say anything.

"Now, boys and girls, I'm going to read you a story until Miss Philomena gets here." Miss Philomena was the school secretary, and she would tell us about first grade.

Miss Immick was in the middle of the story when Miss Philomena came in carrying a big book called a ledger book. You could hear a pin drop.

I didn't care if I ever heard the end of the story!

"Good morning, boys and girls. The following children will please go very quietly and quickly to room two across from Miss Pagnam's kindergarten room. It is Miss Kiniry's room." She started to read out names. I thought I would die.

"Tommy dePaola," she called out. I thought I would faint. I didn't move.

"Tommy, I called your name," Miss Philomena said.

This time I got up and started to walk out of the room. "Congratulations, Tommy," Miss Immick whispered to me as I walked by her.

I went into Miss Kiniry's room. She looked prettier than ever.

"Welcome, children," she said. "And yes, Tommy. We do learn how to read this year."

"When?" I asked.

"Friday," Miss Kiniry answered.

It was Wednesday. The first day of school was always on Wednesday.

We were given our own desks—*real* desks

—with chairs. My desk was in the row next to the windows. I was the first seat. We would always sit in the same place.

I looked around the room. The bulletin boards were all decorated with pictures and words that I couldn't read yet. Across the top of the blackboard stood twenty-six alphabet cards with a capital letter and a smaller letter on each.

First grade was going to be fun!

One of the first things we did was to make a color wheel. Miss Kiniry gave each of us a pencil, a box of school crayons, and a round cardboard milk-bottle top.

"Now, boys and girls," she said, "carefully draw around the milk-bottle top. Make six circles on your paper. Do it just like I have drawn it on the blackboard." Then we had to color in the circles in the right order—red, orange, yellow, green, blue, violet.

It was really something how some of the kids couldn't stay in the lines and how messy they colored. Because I was going to be an artist when I grew up, my color wheel was very neat. Miss Kiniry stuck a gold star on it!

On Friday morning, when I came into my first-grade room, Miss Kiniry whispered, "This afternoon!"

I knew what she meant. I practically flew home for lunch and flew back to school. (We ate lunch at home in those days.)

"Well, Tommy, you are the first one back," Miss Kiniry said as the other kids walked in behind me. She went over to the big activity table in front of the room. There were three piles of books—a yellow pile, a red pile, a blue pile. All the books were the same inside, but each one had a different colored cover.

When everyone was back in their seats, Miss Kiniry handed the books out. She gave me a blue one. I would be in the blue reading group.

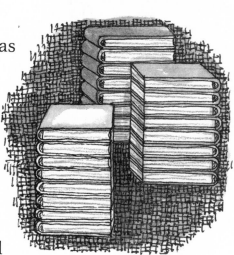

"Now, class, don't open your books until I tell you." I peeked quickly. *Ooops!* The pictures that I saw weren't very exciting.

Then Miss Kiniry went to an easel at the front of the room. It was covered with a cloth. She held her pointer—a long wooden thing with a red rubber tip on it. She took the cloth off. There was a big book just like ours.

"Open your books," she said. She opened the big book. "Now follow along with me." She pointed at the words and read aloud. "See Dick run. Run, Dick, run. Run, run, run. See Dick run."

This is not what I had in mind! By reading I meant, "Once upon a time, in a deep dark wood stood the cottage of the woodcutter."

The next page was no better. "See Jane run. Run, Jane, run. Run, run, run. See Jane run."

I was in trouble. I expected to learn how to read quickly. Get Miss Kiniry to sign the slip that said I could read. Go and get my "liberry" card (that's how we all pronounced *library*) and take out books! You couldn't get your library card until your teacher signed the slip.

So I did a bad thing. I hid the book under my sweater and took it home.

Mom saw the book. "Where did you get that reading book?" she asked.

I answered, "Miss Kiniry said I could take—"

"No, she didn't," Mom said, not even letting me finish. "You stole that book from the school." Now I was not only a boy who didn't know how to read, but I was a criminal. I would have to remember that for my First Confession at St. Joseph's next year. (That's when you told Father O'Connell all the bad things you had done so that you could make your First Communion.)

"Monday morning, young man, you are going to go to school early and confess your crime to Miss Kiniry and apologize to her."

I couldn't get away with anything. Oh well.

Since I had the book all weekend, I decided I would learn to read the whole thing! So, I asked everyone—Buddy, Mom, Dad, Tom, Nana, Uncle Charles, his girlfriend, Viva, Mickey Lynch—what the words were. By Sunday night I could read and remember the words on every page. It wasn't that hard. There weren't *that* many words. See, run, Dick, Jane, Spot, Puff, baby—

So on Monday morning, I confessed my crime.

I apologized. I even cried a little. Miss Kiniry was very understanding.

"But," I added, "Miss Kiniry, I learned how to read."

"Really, Tommy?" she said.

"Yes. Sit down," I said.

She sat down and I read the entire book to her. And guess what Miss Kiniry said?

"Well, Tommy, that is so great that I am going to sign your library card slip right now!"

Mom took me to the library the next day. I got my very own library card and took out one book. (I wanted to take out three, but that's another story.)

Life was wonderful. My baby sister was healthy and happy. Our new house and neighborhood were great. I would be six in a week or so. Dancing school was starting up again. I was learning to read and I had my library card.

I was ON MY WAY!!!

(There's more coming!)

Tomie dePaola is known for his popular picture books about his childhood, including *Nana Upstairs & Nana Downstairs* and *The Baby Sister*. He is the recipient of a Caldecott Honor and the Regina Medal. *26 Fairmount Avenue*, his first chapter book and the first book in this series, was a 2000 Newbery Honor Book.